CW01521300

WATERS OF THE HEART

Edited by

Heather Killingray

First published in Great Britain in 2003 by
POETRY NOW
Remus House,
Coltsfoot Drive,
Peterborough, PE2 9JX
Telephone (01733) 898101
Fax (01733) 313524

HB ISBN 1 84460 914 6
SB ISBN 1 84460 915 4

FOREWORD

Although we are a nation of poets we are accused of not reading poetry, or buying poetry books. After many years of listening to the incessant gripes of poetry publishers, I can only assume that the books they publish, in general, are books that most people do not want to read.

Poetry should not be obscure, introverted, and as cryptic as a crossword puzzle: it is the poet's duty to reach out and embrace the world.

The world owes the poet nothing and we should not be expected to dig and delve into a rambling discourse searching for some inner meaning.

The reason we write poetry (and almost all of us do) is because we want to communicate: an ideal; an idea; or a specific feeling. Poetry is as essential in communication, as a letter; a radio; a telephone, and the main criterion for selecting the poems in this anthology is very simple: they communicate.

CONTENTS

MUM

Always there with a gentle smile,
Or loving comforting word,
Helping us along the way
In this busy world.
Looking after all our needs,
Sharing joys and sorrow,
The same always, yesterday -
Today and tomorrow.
Through childhood to -
Troublesome youth,
We're taught right from wrong,
We learn to tell the truth.
When we're fully grown
The love is still given free,
To see us on our way
Through life to eternity.

E M Gough

A VERY GOOD SAMARITAN

Megan is, a very good Samaritan
Always ready to help a neighbour
She will take by car a friend to hospital
Get food in, if a neighbour is taken ill
She bothers about other people's welfare
Though she herself, is not really well
What a delightful person to know
She gives others the inclination to do the same
Megan is, a very good Samaritan.

Alma Montgomery Frank

PAUL

(Dedicated to my son Paul who died 1985 aged 25)

I once had a son called Paul, who was 6 foot tall,
So handsome, big and strong, with looks of a film star,
Ebony eyes, long black hair, my pride and joy,
The apple of my eye, he could run like a deer,
Dive and swim like a dolphin,
A character and personality,
So rare and comical and funny, he could make me laugh and cry,
When my hand was in his, I felt 10 foot tall,
All eyes would be on him even in rags, he stood out in a crowd,
He was a tower of strength, my pillow of love,
I could move a mountain with him beside me,
He protected me so many times from danger,
But one day in spring, when he was just twenty,
He packed his bags, and said I'm off to London,
Big city where he thought the pavements were paved with gold.
Against my advice, my happy go lucky carefree sunshine
Son set out to earn his fortune, but an evil needle took his life.
Whilst in the midst of manhood still in his prime,
The devil took over and my Samson lost his life in Leicester Square.
His favourite haunt, my son died as he lived,
Everyone's friend. To know him was to love him.
Never to forget, that night the heavens opened,
The lightning struck, the wrath of the devil struck my sunshine,
My son was no more, the gates of heaven opened,
Two angels stood aside and the Lord came down and
Said 'Come Paul' and took him to his promised land.

Pauline Hall

BEST FRIENDS

We go back a long way
You and I the years have flown
And here we are
The mature years
Sometimes we creak and moan
But fun is how
We spend our time
Our humour to the fore
Take us near the shops
Somehow our hearts begin to soar
Gathering a thing or two
We never mean to buy
Always think of others
Most importantly we try
Our friendship hasn't waned
Our sense of humour
Still shines through
And friends like you and I
Will always feel as best friends do.

Jeanette Gaffney

FOREVER A FRIEND

Oh, why did you leave me
Alone like you did?
Our friendship was young
Oh, why did you leave me, you ne'er have should.

Things I want to say,
To question why
Never again will you see
With your eye.

I want to ask you
Your opinion is good
But never before me
Again you stood.

Things unquestioned
And never told
I wanted to ask you
Have never been solved.

New friends I have, good and true
But the questions I ask them
Are not the same
I asked you.

Angela Humphrey

ANGEL OF BEAUTY

Only an angel of beauty
Like you my dear Linda Marie
Can make my life happy
And my heart beat faster and faster.

Only an angel of beauty
Like you my dear Linda Marie
Makes me feel so lucky
So very, very lucky
To have an angel of beauty
Like you
As a very good friend and wife.

For you were always there
When I needed you
You were there to hold me tight
Through the long and cold winter nights
And you were always there
To walk hand in hand with me
Through the countryside and trees
And along the golden surf kissed beach
As the golden sun once more
Rose slowly up into the cloudless and bright
Angel blue sky.

Donald John Tye

A HEAVEN SENT MESSAGE

I'm sitting here with pen in hand, trying to recall,
the mum I've known throughout my life, a stranger after all,
They say time wipes out memories, I can't remember much,
the little hugs and kisses, or a tender loving touch.
The plasters placed upon my knee, no tears were kissed away,
she always seemed so busy, it was just another day.
My childhood memories vary, I know she did her best.
Yet when I hear of others mine was different from the rest.

Maybe I forgot the times, we visited the zoo,
the little treats, the holidays, I can recall a few.
She kept me clean, always fed, put clothes upon my back,
though strict with rules; she never flinched should I deserve a smack.
She brought me into this wide world, I grew up strong and able,
to stand up on my own two feet, and sit at any table.
I know she did her very best, the only way she knew,
my feet are firmly on the ground, I've learnt a thing or two.

At Christmas time I got my share of toys and books and gifts,
summers in the meadows, an odd picnic or day trip,
To visit Gran and Grandad sitting in the big armchair,
eating a biscuit from the tin, or an apple or a pear.
I wonder if her childhood, was different or just the same,
she seldom - showed affection, and rebuffed it when it came,
Her birthday she would read the card but not accept a hug,
if you put your arm around her it was rejected with a shrug.

But still she was my mother, the only one I knew,
and now I cannot talk to her and ask Mum how are you?
So I'm writing you this letter, and I'll leave it on your grave,
with the roses from the garden, that last winter you did save.
I hope an angel then collects it, takes it back to you,
then you can read the things I've said, for in my way I did love you.
You always were my mother, and you're resting now above,
so I will close this letter, to catch the angel's post with love.

Kathleen Townsley

A TOAST TO MUM

I drink a toast to you Mum
To say thank you for all you've done
For just being there Mum
The one and only you.

What would I do without you?
I would miss your words of encouragement
When you say, that suits you Carole
I drink a toast to you Mum.

Thank you for being you. Mum.

Carole A Cleverdon

THE BEST DAYS OF DUDLEY MOORE

They called him cuddly Dudley,
Because that's what he was,
He always made me laugh,
With Peter Cook as his other half,
He was always a good actor,
Acting the fool, memories of him
Will always live with me.

Roger Brooks

HEALING JOURNEY

Through chemo
I walked beside
My friend,
She walked with me,
Was I the healer
Or was she?
I watched
As crystals spun
Their energies
Into her being;
Our inner eyes
Were calm and seeing.
Felt chemical
Harsh smells dissolve,
Experienced
Bright worlds of light
On inner planes.
Within this fight
Came guidance -
Gardens - Japanese,
Calm treescapes,
Polished stones of green
Spiralled into
A place unseen.
Worlds within
Worlds, we travelled
And laughed,
Crossed dark stones of pain,
Retraced our steps,
And met up once again.

Janet Morgan

REMEMBERING FRIENDS

Now I am older, I care to remember a
friend at school, I will never forget
her face, her hair, her smile, her laugh, will be
with me everywhere.

I have to move, I told her
although our friendship still remained, for at least
a year or two, longer, not the memory just remained.
I will never forget the time we shared, I can say
she was the best friend a girl could ever have,
but years have come and gone since then, I have
heard of some troubles she's had.

I wonder if she ever remembers me, or has life
for her been that bad, or is it things that happen in our lives,
just makes me remember our friends, because we
were young and innocent then, who hadn't lived or
made a past.

I hope you're still out there my dear friend,
still managing to make people laugh,
I shall hold onto my memories, then until
we see each other once again.

Lynda Hopkinson

PROUD AT NINETY-TWO

You are so proud that you have reached your ninety-second birthday.
I know you would like to reach a hundred, to get a card from the
Queen, so come on Flo let's celebrate your ninety-second birthday,
let's have a drink and have some fun, then we can sing to Foster
And Allen, and we can sit and reminisce all about your past.
I sit and listen with sheer delight to all the things you tell,
the time you spent all your money to buy that little house in Rainford
it was worth it you said, and the time your mum shouted
at you for reading in the bath and falling asleep,
and when you joined the WAF's you told the girls you were
twenty-five and you were really thirty. But now you're proud
to tell everyone that you are ninety-two, you're only young once
Flo, so sing and shout and celebrate your ninety-second birthday.

Janette Whitthall

DEAR MOTHER

You taught me to laugh
to talk and to smile
you taught me to walk
to run a mile.

Maybe as I've grown
I've been no angel
we all learn by mistakes.

Through bad times and good times
you are always there
the tears that fell, you wiped
you wrapped your arms around me
to ease my breaking heart.

You've guided me through life
reassured me when times got hard
I look up to you
my heart is full of pride.

For dear mother
you're the sunshine
wrapped around my heart
my love for you glows
like an English rose.

For I am proud to have a mother
so beautiful in and out
so warm and loving
precious and sweet
I could never be without.

Deborah Sharples

MY MUM

The pain I carry in my heart,
Is because you went away,
We should never have had to part,
I wish you could've stayed,
It broke my heart when you did go,
The pain, even after eight long years, is still so raw,
I try to picture you, sitting there,
But you won't, not anymore,
I try to think of your voice,
Giving me sound advice
And putting me on the road to life,
From baby, to teenager, a mother, and wife,
I love you Mum, I miss you so,
How I wish, you never had to go.

Diane Campbell

I WISH YOU ALL THE HAPPINESS THAT LOVE CAN BRING

(To Catherine and Andrew for their marriage - September 11th 1993)

I wish you all the happiness,
and all the joy that love can bring.
May all your dreams come true
in everything you do.
I wish you all the happiness
that love can bring.

I'll hold you in my arms
with all your lovely charms;
Because I love you;
Because I love you.

I'll hold you in my arms
with all your lovely charms;
Because I love you;
Because I love you.

When all the world is ours,
and stars shine just for you,
and the moon is full of love.
I wish you all the happiness
that love alone can bring.

John Wiltshire

30TH SEPTEMBER 1987

All these years we've been together
Through good and bad we've survived
From Hell to Heaven you've supported me totally
I can only hope I've been there for you too.

From days of freedom,
To days of commitment
From young lovers, to parents we've developed.

Always together, always supportive,
Even in the darkest days we knew we'd go on
Our family our most cherished achievement
Anything we'd do for them we both know.

But underlying always the one fact so true
On the night we met I said we'd be together forever
To this day in my heart I still believe that's true.

No matter what else has happened
No matter how many tears have flowed
Deep in my heart you'll always belong

I drive you insane at times,
We know it goes both ways
But that's why we're together
It keeps us alive.

The most precious gifts imaginable
You gave to me
Our two beautiful daughters
Our lives they have always been.

So now all I want to say
Are three words I've never shy'd from saying
And now I've written them
In my own 'rambling' way

I love you.

Agnes Neeson

ANNA

(A poem to a lovely girl)

She worked so hard
Every day of the week,
The market girl from Norfolk
I loved her so.
Watched her ambidextrous movements
Move the chocolate and cereal boxes to
Another place all the time.
I want to care for you Anna
I said to myself -
'Men are strange species'
She said to me.
But she was the princess
I wanted to cherish
And I bought her a fashionable cross
To wear from a high class shop
To protect her from evil.
And maybe if I asked her nicely
She would warm to me and want
To go out with me.

Gerard Allardyce

MOTHER

Small things teach me your presence
the iced-lemon peace rose, alone
in winter bloom, the busy robin
flitting in the gathering gloom
and . . . your silent watching
ever watching . . . at my door, when
my head is buried in the papers
on my desk . . . always there.
I never raised my head to let
you know I was aware, yet
silently made note that forever
I would treasure those moments.
I still do. Now I know you had
sensed as well . . . that we both knew.

Evelyn Leite

UNTITLED

I will protect you,
I will save you every time you fall,
You're my beautiful angel,
I am your guardian angel,
I'll be your hero,
Solve all your problems,
Kiss away your pain,
Let you feel my love,
As I hold you close,
As we hold each other,
I hide my teary eyes,
Not letting you see my pain,
The pain I feel when I watch you suffer,
When I'm powerless to help you,
The distance is so far,
But our hearts remain close,
I never want you far from my arms,
As I will never wander far from yours,
Life is full of sharp words and mindless people,
I hope my love shields you from that,
Let my love surround you,
Like my lips when I kiss you softly,
I put my faith, trust and life in your hands,
Not feeling safe until you become part of me,
I want you inside me and beside me,
You're my guardian angel,
As I hope I am to you.

I stand in-between the two of you,
as you each hold half of my heart,
Not knowing which way to look,
which way to turn,
Smile to one,
Cry to the other,
I have a past with one,
A future with the other,

Love for them both,
One will lead me to happiness,
The other to sadness,
I take the risk,
Suffer the consequences,
I will not know if I make the right choice,
Because I will never know life with the other.

Why can't I trust you?
What am I holding back for?
Why do the words 'I trust you'
seem so big in my eyes,
why does my heart ache,
when I'm so sure you're lying
but in truth,
you tell no lie
I can't look you in the eyes
see your honesty and faith in me
behind your skin
something stops me
from believing
cuts through my mind like glass
corrupting my angelic views of you
pulling me back
set free my doubtful ways
let me believe every word you say
I'll rid myself of all doubts in my mind
and finally say
I trust you

Stacey Davis

A LINK

Our grandson arrived unexpectantly
He had promised before but . . .
We reminisced about his younger days
Like old times, with inner pain
I often say why Lord is he into the drug scene?
We're so concerned about the lifestyle he leads
But he's aware he's still loved
In spite of these things . . .
See you, when he got up to go
Whispered, 'Love you Gran'
Before walking down the road
Thankfully we're still close
This vital link will never be broke
For our unconditional love and prayer
Went with him
Wherever he might roam

Chrisie Osborn

THE QUEEN

The Queen
She's very keen
To do the right thing for her nation
There is the sweetest sensation
When she's seen in public
We all so love it
Elegance is her way
When we pray we say
Long live Elizabeth Regina
There is none who is finer

Denise Walters

THANK YOU

Thank you.

Two mere words my friend, that I shall forever cry out to you
from my heart
from my soul,
from my mind.
Words that I would long to tell you once more to your face -
if only God were that kind.
If ever I meet with you once again, in a land unknown, at a time unseen
I will tell you
in warm embrace
you were the best friend a person could have been.

Mike Barlow

GRANDMA

Why so cruel?
He took you away
Velvet hands
And snow white hair
Grandma you touched my soul today

If I listen carefully into the silent night
I can hear your voice telling me everything will be all right
Oh Grandma you left my world so bare
When I'm sleeping I can feel you stroke my hair
Singing lullaby that took me there
To the place and land of pure clear air

But Grandma why did you go away?
I wanted you to stay forever
A childhood dream - slightly selfish
But oh how I miss your touch today.

Ailsa E M Paris

A Mother's Love

May the stars shine,
On dear mother of mine,

Like the softness of a rose,
From all the scents of Heaven,
May the flame
In her heart
Keep on glowing,
For the love that she
Keeps on showing.

May the stars keep on shining,
On a dear mother of mine.

A Bhambra

To My Dad

What you gave to me
Is realised in the passing of time,
Memories that pop into focus
At unexpected moments;
Thinking of things I enjoy
Encouraged by you -
Listening to beautiful music,
Classical, with eternal appeal,
Long walks
Down country lanes, from
One village to the next,
Cricket - whether England win or lose,
(I loved that day at Lords)
Playing word games,
Though I could never beat you,
Or do your Guardian crossword!

Now, your physical presence is
No longer here,
It's too late to say thank you
Face to face,
But know that all you did and were
Is forever appreciated,
You are loved!

Jane Otieno

RECIPES FOR LIFE

My dear little mum was a stikler for etiquette.
Sandwiches (never sarnies) were always served with a serviette.
Her house, like her, was spic and span, spiders were banned.
Dusters and polish were always to hand incase some friend dared
to casually, unexpected but always welcome called.
Her 'Be-ro' book of recipes was her only reference book
as well as being a 'Mrs Bucket' she was a lovely cook.
She hated anything vulgar and often wrote to the Queen.
'She's a mother just keen on morals, hates anything obscene . . .'
She wore her hats with such panache, her shoes were always high of
heel and always made of leather, but the grandmother in her caught
three buses to see my children in any inclement, foul, cold weather.
She taught us how to dance, the quickstep, tango and rumba.
Table manners, housewifery and love,
her sense of humour on dark days,
her strengths runs through my blood.
Would to only have her here with me now if I could.
She's in Heaven now looking over me, with Aunty Edna, Uncle Lol,
no doubt bossing them about and making sandwiches for tea?
Her recipe for Xmas cake is a secret family thing and is passed down
from mother to daughter,
I think if her each festive celebration as we all sigh . . .
'Not as good as Nanna's.'
My 'sarnies' are cut into quarters and served as she'd have done,
I wish she was here to scold me as I sometimes forget my manners.
So Mother I write this poem for you, I'm just making some lemon curd.
I feel you're scolding me . . . 'I did sterilise the jars.'
'I did scrub my hands.' Was that her laughing? Oh, that's absurd?

J M Hefti-Whitney

MY HEART GOES OUT TO YOU

Dearest friends, my heart goes out to you
Losing David I know what you're going through
The pain it brings no one knows how to bear
Wish I could help and take a share
But now my friend David is now at rest
May sound awful, but it's now for the best
No more pain, he can sleep in peace
David gave us warmth with the love he released
My friend David, I will miss you along with lots of other people
    You will never be forgotten
    Rest in peace.

Anne Davey

JOHN LENNON

I'd love to have known you
    John
        the world's friend
because that's what you were all about
            No doubt
      you loved your people
  we loved you too
          but a fool's a fool
to play his own game
  make his rules
and if (by chance)
        he shouldn't win
    (and Hell should hold a seat for him)
        it's his own ruin
But not you! Why you?
  You played fair . . .
      It was all you asked
        (eternal peace)
for war to cease
  and the world to love
You kept your secrets
        behind your mask
      the face of a clown
      letting it go
  in the words of a song
        but this song's for you
John
  because you had the power
    to love them all
      (I can't even love one)

Renée Wallen

MISSING YOU
(For Richard)

There is now
This awful emptiness in our lives,
An unfillable space
Where you used to be,
The last born,
Indeed, always the baby
Of our family of three.

My son, why did you
Take your leave
So very suddenly
From those who now grieve,
Bereft and heartbroken,
Mourning a loss
Impossible to replace,
Almost too difficult to bear?

And what of the dogs
You homed and walked,
Now a leaderless pack
Of greyhounds who've seen
More energetic days,
Though none quite so sad,
A retirement in your sunshine
Has dimmed to endless shade?

For ourselves, we have memories,
Those affectionate hugs now
Never to be, that shy smile
We won't ever see,
A rich legacy of love
That overwhelms yet sustains,
A symptom of grief,
An antidote to pain.

Andrew Farmer

MISSING YOU

There is sorrow acute in the home of O'Donnells
For Jimmie, our daddy is laid low in the clay.
The dark clouds of sorrow gathered over our household
When we saw the deep pain that furrowed his brow.
While we watched by his bedside our bright hopes soon vanished
The call from on High was much stronger somehow.

We knew in our hearts that our darling was dying
Meenawarra's green fields would ne'er see him again.
No more to Ballyharry would he go in the evening
To visit his birthplace where his first steps he took.
We won't see his face by the window at sunset
As he waited our coming when our week's work was done.

We laid him to sleep in the grave of his forebears
And the green sod of Bocan rests light on his breast
Let us not weep for a husband and father
Who shall be waiting to greet us in Heaven on high
May the soft winds of Redford and his own beloved Ardban
Caoin a sweet Irish lament o'er a true Gaelic son.

Brigid O'Donnell

GRANDER BILLY

(Dedicated to William Hugh Turner 1914-1996)

I miss you, like
The world would
Miss its morning dew,
You were one of
The few, who knows
What life's about,
I miss you, I miss
Your cuddles, your
Eskimo kisses, your
Kind advice, the
Time you gave for
My troubles,
I miss the joy and
Laughter you gave,
I could go on, yet
All I can do is say
I really do love
And miss you always.

Paula Natalie Burgess

YOU

You were taken from this world,
Without any time to speck.

Time is of the essence,
But we sometimes ignore our thoughts,
Push them to the back of our minds,
And we are only left with,
I should of told you.

So many things I wanted to say,
Oh how I wish time could stand still,
Just for one more day.

Ann Lacy

FOR MY SPECIAL ANGEL . . . (ALBERT WINDRIDGE)

How do you mend a broken heart?
I wish that I knew,
Because my heart's been broken Dad,
Since the day that we lost you.

People tell me to stop crying,
They say that it's time,
But I wish that they could reach inside,
And tell this heart of mine.

You see it still aches for you,
And the teardrops still fall,
But knowing that you will never see my children grow,
Is the hardest thing of all.

You never complained about anything,
You took it all on the chin,
You kept telling us that you weren't going anywhere,
You didn't want to give in,

But your heart stopped beating,
And we knew that you had to go,
Heaven gained an angel,
But our family lost its brave hero.

So tell me how to go on,
How to dry this tear,
Because I don't know how to Dad,
Now that you are not here.

I miss you so much Dad xxxxx

Kim Laskey

THE KING

Elvis the trucker
The one who was born
To be a King
Crunching the gears
Singing real rock and roll
As he cruises from coast to coast.

Elvis cut a record
The rest is history,
Enter on the stage
The messiah, the showman of the new age

Elvis the pelvis
The censors censure
With a triple X certificate
The girls adore the one
Who was born to be
The great rock and roll King

Every man anywhere
Wanted to look like the King
To dress like the King
To talk and act like the King
Every dame dreamed of being
His one and only rock and roll Queen

Elvis has a magnetic core
From the charisma of his soul
Elvis moved with the grace
Of an African jungle cat
Some even say
That his soul, is the core
Of dark, black Africa

Karma, karma the buckled wheel
Of Lord Karma keep rolling on and on
What if? What if?
Elvis inherited King Midas' legacy of gold?
Only sweet Jesus may know.

Blue, blue, blue suede shoes
Sex and drugs rhyme
Like sugar and spice with rock and roll
Elvis wrote his name, on the wall
In the hall of fame
The one who was born to be King.

T Lawrence

ELIZABETH BOWES-LYON - A LOVE STORY

Born to the family clan of Bowes-Lyon,
An infant of destiny grows into childhood,
Fairest of face and vivacious of temperament

When war comes, she puts aside games and enjoyments,
Her home is transformed to a military hospital.
She tends, with compassion, the sick and the wounded.

War horrors cease and the guns become silent.
A debutante now, she emerges in lov'liness
And attracts the attention of shy young Prince Albert.
Determined to win her, he waits with great patience.

Her marriage with 'Bertie' and two little daughters
Makes everything perfect. As Duchess of York she
Fulfils public duties with charm and devotion,
Delighting her husband, her children, her public.
But one day, their 'world' falls collapsing around them,
For 'Bertie' must face he is heir to the throne! With
The greatest reluctance they accept the inevitable.

King George the sixth, with his precious Eliz'beth
Move from their home into Buckingham Palace.
They take up their duties and win much affection.
When war is declared, they stay on with their people,
Consoling the injured and bombed-out East-Enders.

After the peace, and some bless'd years together,
Elizabeth suddenly finds herself widowed.
She picks up the pieces, is titled Queen Mother and
'Magical grandmother, gloriously unstoppable'.
'Incredibly kind,' said Prince Charles, 'and I loved her.'
Now farewell, sweet lady, the pride of your country,
Serene in God's love, with your 'Bertie' forever.

Nancie Cator

SKIPPING BACK

I'm skipping back to crab apple days,
To the scent of a sizzling pan,
To meals in a prison garden
Where Susan and I made plans.
Plans that were daringly dangerous,
Like stalking forbidden ground.
Lying low in the jungle scrub
While the gardener made his round.
Hardly daring to breathe at all,
We watched the monster pass.
We were secret agents
Trespassing prison grass.
Wintertime brought different games,
Windows became our stage.
We hid behind long grey curtains
And I was a king or a page.
A lovely log fire was our footlights,
Created by Susan's dad.
I remember some pumping bellows
And the sparks shooting up like mad!
I remember an extra super tea
With chocolate cake half a mile high!
On the top was American frosting,
When I think of it now I sigh.
And I dream quite a lot just lately
For magic is hard to find.
I have to go skipping back again
To another place and time.

Alan Pinnock

A Special Christmas

It was Christmas Eve 1944, I was eight years old.

Like every other child on Christmas Eve, I was filled with excitement, at what the morning would bring.

After being tucked up in bed I could not sleep!

Pulling the curtain at my bedroom window aside I looked out onto what was known as 'the blackout'!

Not a street lamp was shining. Undaunted, I looked up into the night sky. It was like black velvet, dotted here and there with twinkling stars. I was looking for one particular star, which was said to shine in the east! Apparently, the one which had guided the three kings to the stable in Bethlehem where Jesus was born.

Having no conception of north, south, east or west, at that age I simply scanned the sky, until I found what I perceived to be the brightest star in the heavens. Gazing in wonder at the star I made a wish that this Christmas would be a very special one. With unquestioning faith I just knew, that it would be!

On Christmas Day, I was drawn to one particular object among my presents. It was a long black cylindrical box, with a piece of clear glass, fitted at one end, rather like a camera lens.

Curiously, I looked through the glass, and was astounded at what I saw. To me, it seemed, that fragments of a passing rainbow had been trapped inside of it.

There were many tiny, brightly coloured shapes making a beautiful pattern. I shook it gently and as if by magic, the shapes moved and turned into a different pattern.

Again, and again I shook the box, and each new pattern that emerged was more colourful and magnificent than the last, this was magic indeed!

I was totally enchanted, by this simple inexpensive toy, which gave me hours of pleasure. How many eight year olds today I wonder would respond as I did, to such a simple gift? Especially, in this high tech world in which we now live?

I was told that my strange, fascinating gift was called a kaleidoscope. That gift, which I received over fifty eight years ago made that particular Christmas the one that I will always look back upon as nostalgically magical, and marvellous to remember!

Patricia Whittle

REMEMBER

Remember when bairns had holes in their socks and patches in their pants. Their jerseys too big, some cases too small, that were knitted by old spinster aunts. Remember when water was brought from street taps, bowler hats kept for funerals and all men wore flat caps. It was ham and a salad for everyone's wedding, the same meal for funerals the old folk were dreading.

Remember the means test so grim and degrading. Rickets, tuberculosis then all hope starts fading. When pantries were bare, just water for drinking, what went through men's minds, what were they all thinking? Remember the caller who brayed on the knocker, old Grandad's chest heaving, asleep in the rocker. Baked bread on the window sill waiting to cool, one wage keeping eight small bairns still at school.

Remember the bike that said, 'Stop me and buy one.'
Corner shops with a slate and others that had none.
Clipping rugs made for Xmas unfinished by June
Card games on a Sunday in Mother's front room.
Men gassed in a war that was meant to end all
Others lived on in misery brroken limbs by a fall,
Remember the shed and the fire in the garden
When we all said, 'Eh,' only posh folk said, 'Pardon.'
Remember your dad tired out, worn and dirty.
I remember it well I was born 1930.

Alan McBride

WHEN WE WERE HEROES

Take heed of days gone by.
When summers were endless.
The days seemed bigger, brighter.
The world was clearly more defined.
No room for doubt, for fear.
Questioning the choices we made.
Instead, we lived the games we played.
Soldiers on missions of mercy.
Saving the world.
Back then, when we were young.
When we were heroes.
Brave and true.
Blissfully ignorant of our futures,
The fearless and the foolhardy.
Soldiering on, taking risks.
Watching our backs.
You've saved my life a thousand times,
I've carried you when you've been shot.
Undercover, incognito, saving the world . . .
But nobody noticed, nobody thanked us.
The great things we did when we were kids.
When we were young and fearless . . .
All those many years ago,
When the two of us were heroes.

P Joseph Cullen

AN ENCHANTING EVENING

What a wonderful evening to remember.
To feel young at heart and surrender
Like a child to the fairytale *Sleeping Beauty*
Performed by the Moscow City Ballet.
Who cast a spell over the whole audience.
It was a most enchanting performance.
The stage was beautifully set for this enchanting fairytale.
As in most fairytales goodness prevails.

As a critic I write my report.
The courtiers were handsomely attired.
And all the dancers were admired
As they twirled and pirouetted with charm and poise.
Like perfect wound up clockwork toys.
The lady of the wardrobe excelled at her task.
She had no need to hide behind a mask.
The designer of each and every costume I must praise.
For everyone's eyes were raised
With approval at the pretty delicate colours and shades
Of lavender, pink and gold.
Nothing was harsh, severe or bold.
Only the spell cast in fury by the evil fairy
Who by error had failed to be invited to Princess Aurora's
Christening party.
Each and all I know would certainly agree
That the wicked fairy played her part with excellency.
Her black cloak almost seemed to have wings
And her feet lifted as if on springs.
The orchestral music was an absolute sheer delight.
It was a perfect, wonderful, enchanting night.
A night to remember, it gave such joy and pleasure.

Elizabeth Myra Crellin

SCATTERED MEMORIES

Adrift in the oceans of my mind, I see different places and faces.
Some come back to me like lightning in the dark.
Memories scattered to the corner of the mind, some I will never find.

Standing alone with no one around only memories keep me proud.
I'm not really alone as I think back to the past,
If only the time could last.

Turn back time if I could, to find a scattered memory, which is lost.
I'm not afraid what I may find; after all it's only a scattered memory
Lost to the corners of my mind.

Rick Hardwick

FOND MEMORIES

As a young man I found that playing badminton
Far more rewarding than attending the local Scout group.
Badminton, one of the fastest games to be played
Improved youthful co-ordination,
Sharpened reflexes, refined tactical skills.
Games were mostly played as mixed doubles,
Ladies at the net, men covering the back of the court,
Both trying to out position the opposition.
As weeks went by there was a progression
For couples to become partners on the court,
Each trusting in the other's natural abilities.
The young lady who was my partner
Was agile, fleet, quick to read the game.
Positioned we stood tensely awaiting the opponents' serve
Often I distracted by the beauty of my partner's legs.
Walking home one night chattering about our games
I slipped my arm through hers.
'I don't think so,' she said removing my arm
Then gave my hand a gentle squeeze.
Two weeks later she and her parents
Moved from our village in East Yorkshire,
I often wonder if on that night
She knew that our badminton partnership
Was drawing to a close.
Though I have never seen or heard from her since,
I still have odd moments when I remember
The girl with lovely legs.
No doubt she had long forgotten me
From all those years ago.

David A Garside

SHE IS LOVED

Oh, how we loved her
And in our hearts will ever do
And how she loved us too
We who knew her will live a little more
And then we will go where she had gone before
Leaving behind sorrow and our lives
And the great store of memories too.

Two hundred years hence some people
Wandering near her grave will read:-
'She is loved'
By whom, when, where?
They will think: her ways
Must have been unutterably fair
To be still loved,
And assent is murmured in the changing air
And they will move on,
Loving each other more,
Because she is there.

Paul Gardner

NEW FRIENDS

I never had a Catholic friend except Christine, met through Open
University who said I was lucky not being Catholic, not suffering
From original sin and I joked that I could never think up an original sin
And then I blurted out I'd never had a Catholic friend before
She didn't take offence but returned my weekly invitation, for years
She moved away, then abroad; and wrote even more

And I'd never have had a Mormon friend, until the teacher at the book
Group who'd shared teaching tips with me for weeks, and felt so
Comfortable to be with
Her name was Renee and she bought me an umbrella on a rainy day
And she turned out to be a devout Mormon and still emails from
Far away

And I never had a Muslim friend, except for the one who's married to a
Catholic
Plus two lovely girls I teach, their charming mother, I've lost count,
A few others

And I never had an American friend until Margo, the most insightful
Person I know
Every conversation is amazing. Her field was prisoner counselling,
She listened to dangerous strangers, demanding, 'Am I in any danger!'
I can't believe her latest thing - she's teaching the shy Chinese flirting!

And I've never had a friend who wasn't middle class from a
Small family
Like me, except easy-going Jackie, who willingly drives over to see me
And brings lunch, and has such a complicated, extended family
And chats to me for hours, and has a practical answer for everything
And drives me from London to Wales, and she's happy when
I talk non-stop because it keeps her awake, then
Claims she's equally pleased if I sleep all the way back
Because she's tired and needs to concentrate on driving

And it's a pity I didn't meet Barbara earlier
Because I never had a friend like her when I was younger
A friend who sews and bakes and is expert on everything
I remember lots of practical people who didn't interest me then
More's the pity, what a wasted opportunity. I'm trying to make
Amends, because people I wouldn't have spoken to years ago are
Now my treasured friends.

Angela Lansbury

WARTIME, AS A CHILD

Memories are sweet at times
Fleeting sun spots or shadows . . .
The smell of a flowering currant bush
At the gate of a semi-detached
Down a side road in Sidcup,
My auntie and uncle round the corner
With Great Aunt Augusta (Gus).
My cousin Gill had little pet ornaments
Linked together by thin chains on her bedroom window sill,
And all the Enid Blyton books one could desire
Is that where my imagination comes from?
The Five (including Timmy) eating tinned peaches
In a cave behind a waterfall
While scoundrels are after them?

When family came, Gill played the piano
I flitted around in her white tutu,
My brother, did he hide behind the sofa?
Bombs could be heard, and gunfire
From the battery in Barking Park,
Whilst we had tea on a chenille cloth
On top of the Morrison shelter.
I walked to the C of E primary school
In a white fog, with my grandad
The red letterbox loomed up on the corner
We had our box-like gas masks on our shoulders.
Grandad was an air raid warden wearing his tin hat,
I felt proud beside him!
Dried egg omelettes for lunch, no sugar, no butter
No nearly anything, without our coupon books.
All this is a fragment of snapshots in wartime!

Anne Veronica Tisley

PICTURING THE PAST

I found a painting of you, of us,
a picture I left unfinished.
It was of days gone by, happy days,
before childhood dreams diminished.

Sweet, that's what you were,
everyone used to say it to Mother,
yes, you were sweet, loving and kind
nothing like the other child.

The child whose brow was always furrowed,
the moody child, the thinking child,
the child whose head was always burrowed in the sand.

Remember the sand where we used to play,
just you, me and the tabby.
You were forever neat and trim
and I was always shabby.

Childhood is like a piece of art,
its value increases with age,
it's only when you look back, when
older, you value that precious stage.

I cannot finish this picture,
the picture from our past,
to do so would be to take away
the innocence we believed would last.

So, dear sister, the artwork may be faded,
the picture not at all as clear,
but the price of that wonderful childhood
remains very, very dear.

Sarah Kevern

FIRST CHILD'S ARRIVAL

It was some years ago.
I can remember which year
And Thursday was the day.
It was early in the morning
I had to make my way
To the necessary hospital.

I had looked forward eagerly
To my first sight of you.
The nurse had instructed me what to do,
She made me push harder and harder
Until suddenly an extra jerk by you
Separated you from your mother.

They took my small baby away.
We were both tidied and washed.
Then you were placed in my open arms,
A delightful parcel. I full of smiles
Now held my beautiful child
My head bent over my darling daughter.

Kathleen Goodwin

REMEMBER ME

Lay me to rest when my time has come
Beneath the bows of a willow tree so as it bends
And touches the ground where I lay
It will weep for my eternal soul.

Place at my head no stone engraved with name or epitaph
Where I am laid to rest, as in the shortness of time
Those who read the words, are sooner forgotten,
Who I was and why I passed this way.

Let no sad song be sung as I am laid to rest
As they will be unheard by me
But each say a silent prayer for me
And in that prayer think of me
And the friendship we shared,
For a short moment in time.

Shed no tears in remembrance for me,
But smile and muse at the good times
That we spent in this most beautiful world,
Gather those close around you
And hold them in gentle embrace
And remember me.

David Hall

OLD BROWN FRIEND

Another sleepy eyed dawn in a cold December brings me to shiver
as on I fumble downward.
A glance across at the friendly form, my old brown dog,
still and quiet, nothing untoward I think.
But wait I am at last concerned, she is so still in form, too calm for life.
A grateful friend, a companion second to none, no movement at all,
is this possible with no gentle reassuring lift of cuddly fur.

This then is that moment in time, her heart strong beyond belief
is cradled and limp as is this dawn, the tenacity in life
finally surrendered by weakened limbs and fading lungs
expiring in a whisper through the cold night and alone
as if apologetic and subservient.

Now at last as I comprehend this inevitable scene I stoop slowly down
laden by fear and dread, my fingers close her milky eyes and through
misty gaze stroke the old soft brown dog as if she were a queen.
Soft words I can barely say are mumbled in a voice she knew and loved
without question, memories will in time lessen the reality so finally
stamped on this moment.

John Foster

O LORD

O Lord you
Left us
In the
Lurch.
Without
A crutch
To perch
Our soul
On.
How can
I see
A newborn
Tree.
Without
You
Eclipsing
Me.

Nicola Barnes

I REMEMBER YOU

I remember you
As you used to be,
Always ready to hear my troubles,
Never thinking ill of anyone.
I remember warmth
As it used to be,
Always happy, never sad,
Never crying, only laughing.
I remember you,
Never looking to the past,
Only living for tomorrow.

I remember tomorrow,
No longer there was happiness,
Only heartbreak and misery.
I remember you,
Sincere as always you were,
Gentle and quiet,
That had been you once.
I remember tomorrow,
The time to say goodbye.
I choked on the word.

I remember listening
To you, my darling.
I remember love,
With laughter and sunshine.
I remember you,
So tender and thoughtful,
Understanding and sympathetic,
Never thinking negatively,
Always you smiled, never cried,
Even at the end.

I remember end,
Without you the world was still.
I remember crying
As they laid you down to rest.
I remember us,
Joined together as one.
I remember coldness
Without you, dear.
I remember us,
Kissing under the sun.
I remember love
And the gift of loving
You . . .

C A Keohane

FADING

Here, and waiting for the thrill
Of a call that never comes and maybe never will;
Here, waiting to rejoice
I'd forget the lonely hours
If I could only hear your voice

And if you came
The anguished hours could melt away,
The ready retributions fading faster than the day . . .

I try to steel my mind to think of us apart
Hoping that the sight of you
No longer breaks my heart
I try to recognise the things I shouldn't do
I can't have your desire
By always being there for you

I hate to have to show that I can keep my cool;
To have to play a game of chance
To someone else's rules.
Spending my next time
On the time before with you;
Could there be something wrong
With what I say or do?

Yet if you came
The anguished hours would melt away,
The ready retributions fading faster than the day
Yes if you came
The anguished hours could melt away,
The ready retributions fading faster than the day . . .

Gayna Florence Perry

COME HOME

Come home, come home,
I miss you so.

Sweet little pussy of mine.

It's empty here, where you used to sit
On that comfy little chair by the fire.

I call out every evening,
Just hoping for your return.

Come home, come home,
I miss you so.

Sweet little pussy of mine.

Moira Clelland

FIVE MONTHS ON

It hasn't got any better
Since you went away,
My nights are lonely,
Tears drown each day.
I lay helplessly still,
Crying in my bed,
All those memories of us
Play through my head.
Deep down in my heart,
No one will ever replace
The feelings you brought,
The love of your face.
Five months on . . .
You're still here
In my thoughts
With every tear.
It hasn't got any better.
Without you,
My nights are so lonely,
Days are too.
Five months on . . .
And I still feel the same.
I'll keep wishing you'll come home
And take away the pain.

Janine Williams

THE WILLOW TREE

Your presence stood by the willow tree,
Me running like a crazed fairy
To your arms outstretched
Inviting me to coil my body around your chest.
Your arms would act like an envelope
Me and you together
Under the secure gummed paper.
You always said
You wanted to remain unopened,
For us not to be prised apart
By some stranger's hands.
Those hands did become our reality.
The body that stood complete
Under the weeping branches
Breathing life
Now is ashes,
Scattered beside the silence
Of your eternal companions,
The earth and roots of the willow.
While my fragmented wand marks the spot
Amidst the shaded grass.

Clare Mitchell

MISSING YOU

They told me you were dead.
Just something they said -
It did not register,
Yet I noted the inert figure on the floor, feet splayed,
Face rigid in shock
And I wondered why they had removed your shoes.
Two ambulance men stood by
Watching for my reaction.
But I turned away,
For what was there to say?

In the overcrowded kitchen
Men in uniform came with their questions,
Gently discreet.
Priest and doctor had their part to play
And I, it seemed, was cast as lead,
Yet grief was strangely delayed.

When they came to take you away
I walked in the garden
And marvelled how tidy it had been left,
As if it were some well-laid plan,
Your exit chosen to the day.

A neighbour came with chicken broth,
Brought to sustain the life that was left.
It was the real thing with chicken pieces in it.
Strange that she should have it by
To meet this sad occasion,
Which packet soup would somehow have demeaned.

Ice-calm I talked of ordinary things
And listened in to what I said.
I was not me.
I even laughed and wondered at it,
Yet life must go on, they always say.

But left alone at last
Your absence became real
And then I understood their careful handling.
Such unexpected loss was pain
No drug could ever ease.

Tears came like rain to a parched land
And I could hear them saying,
'It would be better if she cried.'

Brenda Lismer

I HAVE NO NEED FOR SWEET DREAMS

There are no dreams here
 for lonely people.
There are no dreams here
 for me.

I was very young once,
 or so I once believed.
There is now no one
 who dreams of me.

I am alone here
 in my mourning.
I am alone here
 but for my tears.

You were once
 within my heart.
You were here once
 within my dreams.

But I do not dream any more,
And I do not dream of truth.
I do not dream of sweet things,
And I do not dream of you!

There is a void now
 where my heart once beat.
There is a sigh now
 where a laugh had been.

Within me I hear a cry
 of a soul to be released.
And I shall sigh, I cry
 until I am set free.

But I see a light now,
   though so very far away.
The light is ahead now
   and not so close behind me.

The price of freedom is too high
   as I will always be alone,
And even until the day that I die
   I will always sleep alone.

And I do not dream any more,
For in my dreams there was truth,
And I have no need for sweet dreams
For in those dreams I still find you.

Angela G Pearson

MEMORIES

Watching as she arranges the things that she must wear
Admiring the flowers she will put into her hair
I remember that first day I left her at the school
The teas I shed, the way she said she didn't mind at all.

But I did, she was leaving me and starting a new life,
I couldn't bear the thought that she might meet with any strife.

However, she has grown into a beautiful young girl
With married life before her, a future will unfurl
Of exciting and unknown pleasures and I hope some of her treasures
Will be memories of me, whatever may be ahead - this really must
be said.

I will look on her with pride - as the mother of the bride.

Dawn Sansum

MISSING YOU

It is a bright, sunny, frosty, freezing morning.
The sun is low, the trees are dark and tinselled.
Ice crackles. The swans
Aloofly watch the small, neurotic ducks.
Only my breath is with me. My ghost.
I remember how you enjoyed days like these.
Your hand was warm in mine and you
Were warm in my soul. Your chatter never ceased.

I used to love the mornings. I awoke
And left you sleeping still in bed
And brought you tea and watched you
Rub your eyes, like a squirrel
Waking in the spring. You were
Too sleepy then to chatter much.
And then the day of work
Divided us until the evening.

And then you used to tell me everything
In funny, angry, passionate detail.
I miss those people that I never met
And knew so well. I miss
The television that we watched together. I miss
The meals, I miss the holidays, I miss
You snuggling up to me in bed.
I miss hearing you dream.

How did I let you go? How did it come about
That you are lonely somewhere and I
Walk with my ghost on comfortless,
Cold mornings, remembering your chatter

Missing you?

Fred Brown

SONG OF SORROW

Can you hear my song of sorrow,
Can you hear my song of woe?
If I give up my life for you,
Will you even remember me tomorrow?

I never said I was anyone special,
But you all claimed I was the messiah
And when they put me up on that cross,
You thought I let them to save you all.

Somewhere on the hill, you missed the point,
The only one who can save you, is you.
If my dying was to mean anything to you
Don't worship me, don't follow those fools.

Now it's too late, too far down you've gone,
No one can save you from the abyss of oblivion
Hanging on by fingertips on the edge of the precipice
And don't pray for me this time, 'cause I ain't the one.

Can you hear my song of sorrow,
Can you hear my song of woe?
If you don't change it all, today,
Maybe there won't be a tomorrow.

Don't save a day to pray for me,
Don't save a day for my birthday,
Don't save a day to mourn my death,
Don't save a day if you worship me.

David McDonald

THE BIGGEST ISSUE

Six am drinking
Doesn't help thinking
Must be the proof
That my spirit is shrinking

Sat by my phone
With the chances I've blown
Thinking of the girl,
Is she all alone?

The letter is written,
Tried not to be smitten
For all my harsh words
I'm sorry my kitten

That one special night
When we lay huddled tight
Reminds me of my strength
And duty to fight

With heads in the sky
Just you and I,
Under shooting stars
Forever we'll lie

Three words never said,
Except in my head
I hope that she hears them
Before I am dead.

Dhan Whitelock

MISSING MERLIN

No magic in the house
No unexpected ambush
No doors crashing open
No toys to trip over
Without Merlin

No rooms to tidy again
No stray hairs on cushions
No bowls of cat food to tread in
On a night raid to the fridge
Without Merlin

No being woken at dead of night
By the banshee howling of a lonely pet
No joy of snuggling down to sleep
With the deep purr of a contented cat
Without Merlin

No anxious wait in vets' surgeries
For blood test results
No vainly trying to tempt
With favourite foods
Without Merlin

No bitten fingers
Forcing down a pill
No wishing there was a God
To pray to for a miracle
Without Merlin

No welcoming greeting
Returning after the deed was done
Just a huge empty space
And a broken heart
Without Merlin.

Rose L Ashwell

MISSING YOU

In sunshine or storm,
Good times and bad
You always were there.
Sometimes not seen,
Often an echo,
A distant voice
Wisdom once expressed,
Memories to heed.
I never doubted
Your love, your care.
Something so welcomed,
Always there.

O L Groom

GONE AWAY

Today there are more tears
From the dark clouds of your eyes.
The light has faded from your face and
Only the misty, scudding nimbus
Of unexplained fear is left.
You have double-locked every access door
Between my reality and the
Stormy recesses of your mind,
Where now I am only one of many monsters.
And it isn't merely the mental shutters that are down.
Our house is like an island Alcatraz
Of new locks, bars and door chains.
And I try to follow you to places
Where you should not go alone,
Places where I cannot go.
Though I would gladly admit to anything,
I know of no proper sin
To which I can plead guilty.
I have behaved as every woman knows
Every man does
But it has been to your amusement in the past.
You have gone away from me
And I do not know how to bring you back
To the knowledge and safety
Of the old place,
In which I was your only monster.

Ted Harriott

REFLECTION
(To Nana, rest in peace)

There were times in the past
When we did not see eye to eye,
Moments when we could not conform.
Now I reflect, as time goes by,
I don't think I ever expressed
How I truly feel.
It is only now that you're gone
That my thoughts I can reveal.
There was many a moment when we talked for hours,
As you spoke, I sat by your side.
You told of the past and memories you cherished
Of Grandad - it was then that you cried.
We had so much fun together when we danced,
We shared so much in common when we talked,
I shall be forever haunted
As I remember, from you that I walked -
It should have been just 'au revoir',
But it turned out to be 'goodbye.'
Maybe in the end it's for the best,
I shall refrain from allowing myself to cry.
I will always remember you in my heart,
Until my dying day,
You were so incredibly special,
I love you, yes, I love you, the beautiful Hilda May.

Kate Boud (17)

ONE DAY IN SUMMER

It was a lovely day
None like it for a long time
Before or since.
The train, the sun, the walk, the view,
Cider with Rosie
A cool beer with you.

Jackie Goode

BEREAVEMENT

She has gone.
No! She is there
on the stair.
In the bathroom
washing her hair.
Opening her lingerie drawer.

Her cheery greeting
as she comes through
the front door.

Always busy in the garden,
secateurs in her gloved hand.
Her roses glowed
on any exhibition stand.

Her paint brushes
are waiting
to be charmed into life.
Quiet and still
lies her palette knife.

He slides his foot
to her side of the bed.
It is cold.

She *has* gone.
No! No!
She will *always* be there . . .
on the stair . . .

Kinsman Clive

MISSING A STRANGER

I miss you, yet you remain a stranger.
Your face is familiar, but I don't know your voice.
Evidence of your artistry and wit
Is tangible, touching, timeless.

You died when I was 15 months old.
You're the father about whom I need to be told.

I imagine my life if you'd been there:
No childhood frustration; no latchkey kid;
No charity clothes; no second-hand toys;
No being different; no embarrassment.

Above all, more precious than gold,
Not to have lived in an all-female household.

Would I have been more diligent at school?
Better results? A different career?
I may not have been so bored, unfulfilled,
Swifter to find what the world has on offer.

Perhaps I wasn't really wilful and bold,
Just flexing muscles as wings began to unfold.

You'd be proud of my daughters and grandchildren,
All gifted and talented, like you.
They're considerate, hard-working, well-rounded,
Live every day to the full.

You died with your life at a threshold.
We've inherited that life and live it tenfold.

Valerie Catterall

LEAVE ME SILENT

Michael flew out across the rooftops,
We knew where he was going
But could not get there in time.

We did not have to wait long until we saw him again,
In the corner watching our gestures and emotions.
As we tried to say goodbye,
He waved to us across the sky.

Then came the great debate;
In the boot, or on our laps?
Across counties we held him,
Until we could almost smell the sea.
Within sight of the Minster.
We made and broke the circle.

When we got home,
Michael stood behind the television
And watched the children play.
Tonypandy died and we smiled,
A new passenger to join his celestial voyage.
'But how can I voyage,' Michael thought,
'When I am watching TV with you?'

Later in suburbia,
Michael and the infant slept in his son's arms.
The infant gurgled,
'Leave me dead,
Leave me silent.'
The son hears Michael's words
And finally understands.

I miss you Dad,
Goodbye.

Emma Jane Stroud

THE WORLD TO ME

I have yearned, you have spurned.
I don't know why, but when I die
Read this rhyme. It was no crime
To love you so and let you go.

My world collapsed, a momentary lapse,
But in its place I could not replace
The love you gave me. So at my grave
Remember though I loved you so,
To stop the tears and fill the years
I saw the wild as my child.
The love I could have given you
Had you only wanted me to,
Became unfurled to the world
As no one soul could fill the hole
You'd left with me, just like a tree
I grew again and eased the pain
And learned to love and accept love.
I love you still, I always will
And now I'm gone, I'll still go on
And be with you. Another view
Of things I'll see, now that I'm entirely free,
Because you'll always be the world to me.

Joan E Blissett

DENIED THE CHANCE
(For Auntie Barbara)

As you lay in your bed awake,
The cancer, hard to take,
'Only days to live,' the doctor said,
With your family beside you, but I was nowhere to be seen.

I begged to come, but the answer was no.
Your suffering would make me cry,
Was their excuse.
All I could think about was you lying helplessly in your bed,
A picture of you spinning around in my head.

A few days later you passed away,
Your body left, with no life to be seen.
I cried and cried, knowing I would never see you again,
A lot to take at the age of ten.

I will never forget the funeral, I laughed
Because I was so upset.
But I was denied the chance to say
Goodbye.

Matthew Lindsell

YOU ARE NOT THERE

Last night I held you in my arms until moonlight
Faded away, only to awake to find that
You are not there, so I imagine you are there
To dance each step, step by step, just like
When we first met.

So I can imagine it as the first moment
We held each other tight, hoping that
I could se the love that's in your eyes.

But you are not there, but you are not there
Oh why aren't you there, so I can
Imagine you are there, as I can feel the Love
You gave to me when we shared that one single dance.
Which lead to our one time romance.

With each dance we dance, with each kiss we kiss
It was without single care, just like it was when we first met,
But when I awake, you are not there,
Oh why, Oh why aren't you there so I can
Imagine you are holding me in your arms,
Making love to me gently through the night.

That's when you made our love first come alive. So Alive,
Then I awake to find that you are not there, so
I imagine you are there,
Dancing each step, step by step, hoping that I can
Catch a glimpse of the love that's in your eyes.

Paul Wilcox

MAGICAL MEMORIES

I am and have always been a great film fan
But I cannot help but remember past times
When as a child, then a boy, then a young man,
I would greatly love going to the cinema.
Often I would go two or three times a week,
For me, cinemas were magical places.
Sometimes large, ornate buildings on the outside,
Inside was like another fantasy world.
Deep carpets, lovely seats, huge velvet curtains
With gilded fittings and a wide staircase
Which led to an even better balcony,
Then the lights in their changing colours
And at last, the start as the projector whirled.
In the old days, we always got good value.
'A' films, 'B' films, newsreels, all next week's features,
Saying farewell to places in travel films.
Memories of the films I saw still remain.
Our favourite stars thrilled us and were heroes -
Cooper, Bogart, Cagney, Grant to name a few.
Do you remember Errol Flynn? My hero.
I still enjoy going to the cinema,
I still enjoy a good film and good acting,
But even modern block-busters and epics
For me cannot compare with the yesteryears.

Terry Daley

THE URCHIN

The other week in our local newspaper
There was a snap of a class of a small village school,
Taken in the twenties, when I was born.
The first thing I noticed was the number
Of children with bare feet.
One boy had a tie on, but still had bare feet,
He also had the widest smile.
We ran on our bare feet in summer, with napped toes,
But not at school, but I remember cutting
A new bit of cardboard to put in my shoes every morning.
I worked in the building trade most of my life
And remember working at a small village school
With a squad of workmen.
We had a fun game of football with the children
At lunch time, much enjoyed by all, big and small.
One little boy did not take part, he stood to one side watching.
He always wore a little old raincoat,
I thought perhaps he was crippled
Until I saw him walk about normally.
Then one day, I had the answer.
A sudden gust of wind blew his coat up around him
And I noticed he had no arse in his trousers.
The poor little soul, I was so sorry for him.
Poor as we were, I could not remember being like that.
We were shifted the next day and I did not see him again,
But I often thought about him.
You may not think it possible,
But there is always someone worse off then yourself.

James Rodger

BEEHIVES IN THE ORCHARD

The land behind the fence had trees touching
The ground with ripe fruit . . . then hens and the duck
Each day would check its topography, with predilection
Dawn and dusk, while the sun was more tender and inviting
This proud orchard had beehives . . . bees everywhere . . .
Rather docile, if nobody happened to be in their way.
In the late afternoon, my grandma would visit her friends
Then she would go to the shops to buy items for tea
Rice, flower and sugar in bags, oil in one's own bottle
Biscuits by the gram, the same with the butter
Rarer than anything else; I would lie on the roof of
The double shed, under the old apple tree, the one
With twisted branches . . . I would read or look at
The vine grow and dream: extravagant fantasies that
Young girls would weave in their minds have nothing
To do with what might happen to the land – bare now -
Trees touching the ground with ripe fruit is a thing
Of the past . . . I couldn't have known it at the time,
When the proud orchard had beehives and bees everywhere.

Mariana Zavati Gardner

To A Friend

I have just lost a greatly valued friend.
He always gave such sound advice on anything at all
about that which he knew
and that advice was well and usefully received.
The knowledge that he passed on to me,
of things both small and great,
has helped me in a lot of things I did in later life
and made me, I like to think, a better man.
His going has left an aching void
both in my mind and I am sure,
in those of all the others to whom he was a friend.
I'm also sure that his advice, calm logic, comfort,
sense of humour, strength and joie-de-vivre
have all had the same beneficial effect on others
as they had on me.
I've lost a friend. He will be missed.
But not forgotten

David G W Garde

THE FACE OF THE AGED

The crinkled skin is stretched, then loosely hangs
With forehead creased like rippled water
The lined mouth that once knew laughter
Now full of whitened, man-made teeth
Wispy white hair is combed aside
Over balding head, so smooth to touch
The watery eyes that have seen so much
Now with a distant haunted look
Staring unsure through thick, round glasses
The mottled hand wipes a solitary tear
At a flickering memory from yesteryear
Never thinking of the future, never looking forward
Remembering, reminiscing in long ago daydreams
What does he have to look toward?

Jane Lynch

BROTHERS

We lived like brothers
But now you're gone
To that special place
Known as home

We shared together
Some real good times
I sometimes felt
You read my mind

All those secrets
We never told
I'll have to keep
Till I grow old

You so young
And oh, so strong
I always thought
Your time was long

But now you're gone
To a better place
I miss you so
That smiling face

My heart is low
Resistance weak
Without you here
The future's bleak

It sometimes seems
As if I have died
Without your shadow
By my side

So rest in peace
Where you lay
And I won't forget
Those good old days.

Sherland Boyce

MY PAL

We've been pals now
For many years,
We've had lots of laughs
And you've wiped away
My tears.
When I was sick
And in hospital,
You helped me through.
Dear pal, what would I do
Without you,
My dear pal?

Rene Kowalski

ELLIE

When you came into my world that day
It changed a part of me
It made me take a look at life and see it differently
I realised what's important
That love it conquers all
That money's not important
It's family that's all
I never imagined a love like this
I never knew what it could be
But now that you are finally here
It's extremely clear to see
That I have been given this beautiful gift
A gift that's so precious and pure
My beautiful daughter Ellie
I could never ask for more.

Michael McLaughlin

KATIE

There's not a day that does go by
Without us thinking oft
A black and tan with velvet eyes
A face so dear and soft
She was our love, she was our life
She was our dear old mate
Yes, we wish she was back here with us
Our dear old friend Kate.

We never will forget her
But why should we try?
She is always here around us
As all the days go by
Although we never see her
We know that she is there
She knows we love her just as much
And knows that we still care.

So Katie you are now at peace
Away from all your pain
We know we had to let you go
To make you whole again
The good thing about love is
It penetrates everywhere
So goodbye Katie, goodbye our love
We know you are around somewhere.

Jean Hughes

GRANDCHILDREN

The bond is there between you
From the day that they are born
The sunshine and the laughter
Are there at each new dawn.

They ask for nothing but your love
Give so much in return
And from the ways of children
We have a lot to learn.

And when they hold up little arms
For a cuddle or a kiss,
There are no joys in all the world
That can compare with this.

Deirdre Atherton

BY MY SIDE

With the sky so high
And with you by my side,
The rivers could flood,
The mountains could fall,
It doesn't matter if you're by my side.
The sun could shine,
All the money could be mine,
I could lay on silk beds
Draped with diamond nets,
Looking at the moonlight
With a beautiful tide.
It wouldn't be worth a thing
Without you by my side.

Kenny Roxburgh

OLGA

Polio had made her feet odd size
She walked in boots, one three, one five
For a while life was tough but then
She wed and had her only child

People sought her healing touch
When anyone was sick
She saved a child that had turned blue
Because he'd had a fit

As diphtheria its deadly finger shook
In her neighbourhood
With disinfectant and with prayers
She fought it best she could

She dug for victory in World War II
And shared her surplus veg
She kept rabbits for a stew
And chickens for their eggs

She cleared glass and rubble from the house
When bombs were thrown her way
For his mother she wrote the allotted words
To a prisoner in Singapore
The hardships she took in her stride
Till victory came once more

Her grandchildren were her heart's delight
For such a very short time
Her great big heart one day just stopped
And suddenly she was gone
Many years have passed
My tears still fall
You see; Olga was my mum!

Joy Ridgewell

POEMS FOR MY LOVED ONES

I never told you what I really thought
of the way you brought us up.
I'd like to tell you know that I'm older,
that you did a brilliant job.
You took care of me, my sister too,
my brothers and our dog,
you made sure we never went without,
we never hung about.
You are my mother, my father to
my aunt and my nana,
I never missed out on a single thing
because you are my mam.
You lost your son, but you stood strong
for us remaining kids,
I'd like to tell you I cry sometimes,
for you my heart does ache.
So here I am telling you now
how lucky I am that you're my mum.
I will never take for granted
the people that I love.

I never once thought to tell you
of the love I had
for you, my brother, at only nineteen
it was the bitter end,
the night I was told that you had gone.
You had done nothing wrong,
a bit of fun went terribly wrong
and you were the one that paid.
I cried for you for days and nights,
you had gone to a place with lights
that you would be all right
in your second life.

I wish I'd told you just one time
that I loved you through your short-lived life.
If you can only hear me today,
I love you more than words can say.

Michelle Roberts

WHERE LIFE LEADS 1950-1993

I met him at a station,
A chap of twenty-five,
I was just a sweet sixteen,
Was he trying to give me the eye?

My train departed, I headed home
I thought no more of our chat.
A few brief words that's all it was
And that was the end of that.

I took work in a hospital,
Just eighteen years was I.
I worked there until I was twenty-two
Then I left for pastures new.

I went to work in a seaside town,
One Sunday a chap passed by.
He had a chat then went on his way,
Oh well, nice day, goodbye!

But this chap turned up again,
He knew where I worked, you see,
I said, 'What are you doing here?'
He said, 'I've been many miles away.'

He had been a soldier for many a day.
We talked, then we dated,
I remembered his name,
The chap when I was going home on the train.

Fate had brought us together,
But once more we're apart.
I'll find you again one day,
You captured my heart.

Rachel Mary Mills

REG, WHERE ARE YOU?

Do you ever come out?
Do you ever see the light of day?
Now that fickle fame has flowered your way to the stars,
Have you been disowned, confined to a dark, paradoxical place
Where unwanted lives are orphaned or stowed away?
Are you as complex as E L Wisty,
Or as soft and simple as a virgin's kiss?
Being split into two, it doesn't seem to bother you.
Do you exist as a grain of sand,
Does anybody ever ask of you or shake your hand?
If and ever you see the sun, how long is it for?
Five, ten or none?
What happens when enough has reached enough?
Are you once more ushered through the suffocating
                              discriminating door?
Who really are you? Where are you now?
How do you both cope?
Do you ever wonder why?
Do you ever have to lie?
What happens when you die?
Which of you will cry the most?
Which of you will be the ghost?
Something just doesn't fit quite right,
Mr Dwight.

Robert Henry Lonsdale

ISOBEL'S FAGS

I never would have thought
I'd ever see the day
That you'd put your lighter down
and throw the fags away

You'd get up in the morning
cough your fag out of the packet,
fumble your way down the stairs
to the shop . . . for another packet

Making your way to 'the street'
going up the 'Baingle Brae'
stopping just to gasp for breath
cos you'd only got half way

It's good to see you active
enjoying life as it should be
instead of curled up on the couch
like a hamster on one knee

At times you feel forgotten
and the hours are slow to pass
just remember our proud we are
you've done it . . . well done lass!

Marion McGarrigle

JULIE

Her name was Julie
There are many Julies in this world but with other names.
She brightens your day,
Likes you to laugh with her,
Her laughter often a protection against the adversities in her life.

Her bag of money almost always empty,
But her bag of courage always full,
Not decked in diamonds, but a jewel herself.

This girl named Julie and other Julies with other names,
Who pass through my life each day.
Angels in T-shirts.

Iris Robinson

MY SOUL COMPANION

No one knows the bitter grief
For few have seen me weep.
I shed my tears from a broken heart
Whilst everyone is asleep,
For I lost my soul companion,
Whose life was linked with mine.
No one knows how much I miss him,
Now that I travel my life alone.

Ella Wright